M000164935

isbn 0-7948-0720-8

© 2001 U.S. MINT UNDER LICENSE TO H.E. HARRIS & CO.
MADE IN USA

H.E. Harris & Co.
Serving the Collector Since 1916

10   9   8   7   6   5   4   3   2   1

FIRST PRINTING

# THE OFFICIAL U.S. MINT

## STORIES OF THE
### 2001

50 STATE QUARTERS™

© 1998 U.S. MINT

*H.E. Harris & Co.*®
Serving the Collector Since 1916

STATE
QUARTERS

© 1998 U.S.MINT

# PROGRAM

If you flip over any of the 50 State Quarters™ Program coins, you will see that each has a different state design on its tail side (known as the reverse). In 1997, Congress passed an Act that established the 50 State Quarters™ Program. The program calls for the production of five new quarters every year for ten years. These commemorative quarters honor each state by featuring a symbol of its history, and are issued in the order that the state accepted the U.S. Constitution and entered the Union.

The many changes in the quarter's design are historical firsts, and are especially noteworthy considering how little the quarter has changed since its birth. The first quarter was minted in 1796, and was originally made of silver. The Mint Act of April 2, 1792, called for the quarter design to feature the date the quarter was minted, the word "Liberty," and an image representing liberty. The image chosen was Lady Liberty, a woman in long robes with gently flowing hair. For over 115 years, she represented the idea of liberty on the quarter's front (called the obverse). Although the style of Lady Liberty's dress and hair changed over the years, it was not until George Washington's 200th birthday in 1932 that the first president replaced Liberty on the obverse of the 25 cent coin.

From the beginning of the 50 State Quarters™ Program in 1999, through its end in 2008, the reverse of the coin will change 50 times. Each coin will not only represent a part of our nation's remarkable past, but will also be a piece of history itself.

# NEW YORK

**Capital:** Albany

**State Flower:** Rose

**State Tree:** Sugar Maple

**State Bird:** Bluebird

**Land Area:** 47,224 sq. mi.

**Rank in Size (Land Area):** 30th

**State Song:** "I Love New York"

**Largest City:** New York City

**Statehood Date:** July 26, 1788

**Nicknames:** Empire State

**New York was named after England's Duke of York.**

The Statue of Liberty welcomes arrivals to America as they prepare to disembark in New York Harbor.

# NEW YORK: EVER UPWARD

Native Americans were the first people to live in New York more than 11,000 years ago. Men hunted animals with spears made from sharpened stones, while women gathered plants and farmed the land. In 1524, Giovanni da Verrazano, an Italian sailor who worked for the French, became the first European to explore New York. He was followed by Henry Hudson, an English sailor who worked for the Dutch, in 1609.

Upon seeing the beaver and mink furs worn by the Native Americans, the Dutch realized that this new land was rich in trapping and trading possibilities, and they began settling the area. Gradually, the Dutch displaced the Native Americans and controlled "New Netherland" (as they called the region) until 1664. Then the British took over and renamed the land "New York" after the king's brother James, Duke of York. These early explorers recognized New York's value right away, and so did our first president, George Washington. Upon setting eyes on the land in 1784, at a time when it was neither populous nor wealthy, he declared that New York would become the "seat of empire." His prediction gave New York the nickname the Empire State.

# GATEWAY TO FREEDOM

New York has welcomed more newcomers than any other port in the country. Look on the reverse (or tails side) of the new quarter, and you will see the words "Gateway to Freedom" beside one of the most familiar symbols of freedom in the world—the Statue of Liberty. Lady Liberty's official name is Liberty Enlightening the World. Her torch, held high above New York Harbor, has lit the way for the millions of immigrants who have come to America in search of a better way of life. A gift from the people of France to the people of the United States, the Statue of Liberty arrived in New York in 1884, boxed in 214 crates. This enormous hammered copper statue stands 305 feet tall and weighs 255 tons. Imagine what an awesome site this shiny symbol of freedom must have been for the more than twelve million immigrants, sailing into port after a long journey at sea, whose first glimpse of America was Lady Liberty.

To this day, New York City has the most diverse population in the country. The city thrives on the energy, ideas, and ambitions of newcomers trying to fulfill their dreams. In addition to celebrating this uniquely American immigrant experience, the New York quarter recognizes the state's importance as a gateway to the rest of the country. Behind the image of the Statue of Liberty is an outline of the state with a line tracing the state's chief waterways, the Hudson River and the Erie Canal. After eight years of construction and much public criticism, the Erie Canal opened in 1825 and launched a new era of growth in the Empire State. Many people settled along the banks of this 363-mile canal. It became the main route for trafficking goods, as delivery was speedy and cheap. Just as the Statue of Liberty welcomes newcomers "yearning to breathe free," this passage between the Atlantic seaboard and the midwestern frontier cleared the way for westward expansion.

## NOTHING BUT THE TRUTH

Isabella Baumfree was born in 1797 in Ulster County, New York, where she worked as a slave in a Dutch household. After gaining her freedom in 1827, Isabella moved to New York City, where she underwent a spiritual transformation that led her to speak out on behalf of women's rights and against slavery. She changed her name to Sojourner Truth (a sojourner never stays in one place for very long) and began traveling around the country proclaiming, "Children, I talk to God and God talks to me." Despite the fact that she could not read or write, Sojourner Truth was a very moving and powerful speaker. At one women's rights convention in Akron, Ohio, in 1851, she said, "If the first woman God ever made was strong enough to turn the world upside down all alone, these women together ought to be able to turn it back and get it right-side up again. And now that they are asking to do it, the men better let them."

## ROLL OUT THE BARREL!

Majestic Niagara Falls was formed 12,000 years ago, when glaciers moved north, pushing water from Lake Erie over a ridge located on the border of western New York and southeastern Ontario, Canada. The American Falls are 182 feet tall and 1,075 feet wide, while the Canadian Falls, also called the Horseshoe Falls because of its shape, are 187 feet tall and 2,220 feet wide. Soft shale and limestone make up the natural bedrock. With the constant flow of water at a rate of 75,000 gallons per second, large chunks of bedrock have tumbled to the base of the falls over time. Geologists predict that erosion (the wearing away of the rock) will eventually turn Niagara Falls into a chain of sloping rapids.

A number of daredevils have attempted to go over the falls in a barrel. Some lived to tell the tale, while others plummeted to their death. The first person to conquer the falls was Annie Taylor, a 63-year old school teacher from Michigan. On October 24, 1901, she climbed into her airtight wooden barrel and took the plunge. Seventeen minutes later, Annie emerged from her barrel very bruised and battered and said, "No one ought ever do that again!"

# HOT DIGGITY DOG!

The all-American hot dog and hamburger were both invented in New York. The brothers Frank and Charles Menches of Hamburg, New York, made the first hamburger for the Erie County Fair in 1885. Around the same time, Charles Feltman invented the hot dog at his Coney Island restaurant.

# NORTH CAROLINA

**Capital:** Raleigh

**State Flower:** American Dogwood

**State Tree:** Pine

**State Bird:** Cardinal

**Land Area:** 48,718 sq. mi.

**Rank in Size (Land Area):** 29th

**State Song:** "The Old North State"

**Largest City:** Charlotte

**Statehood Date:** November 21, 1789

**Nickname:** The Tar Heel State

**North Carolina was named for England's King Charles I.**

North Carolina's Quarter honors the Wright brothers and their first powered airplane trip in 1903 at Kitty Hawk.

# NORTH CAROLINA: TO BE RATHER THAN TO SEEM

North Carolina was claimed by the English in 1629 and named *Carolana*, meaning "land of Charles" in Latin, in honor of King Charles I. His son Charles II changed the spelling to Carolina in 1663. When the colony was divided in 1710, the southern part was called South Carolina and the northern region became North Carolina. Because the northern settlements were older than those in the south, North Carolina earned the nickname "The Old North State."

But North Carolina's best-known nickname is perhaps "The Tar Heel State." Tar, which comes from the slow burning of long-leaf pine tree stumps, was the state's main product in colonial times. During a fierce battle of the Civil War, the soldiers who were supporting the North Carolina troops retreated, leaving them to fight it out alone. Although the North Carolinians won the battle, the regiment that fled was sure they had been defeated and greeted them with the question: "Any more tar down in The Old North State, boys?" The brave soldiers replied that they would give them some to put on their heels to make them stick better in the next fight. When General Lee heard of the incident, he said, "God bless the Tar Heel Boys," and the nickname has "stuck" with the state ever since.

# FIRST FLIGHT

The image on the North Carolina quarter celebrates one of the most exciting events of the 20th century—the first successful airplane flight. Wilbur and Orville Wright first took an interest in flying in 1896, upon reading of the death of a famous German glider pilot. Although they were troubled by the fact that so many great minds had made so little progress, the Wright brothers were inspired by the fact that they had as much chance as anyone of succeeding.

Wilbur wrote to the Smithsonian for research materials in 1899 and began reading everything that had ever been written on flying. He and Orville began experimenting with different airplane designs, graduating from a kite to a winged sled and, finally, to their famous biplane. They chose Kill Devil Hills near Kitty Hawk, North Carolina, as the site of their first test flight because the winds were steady and the sandy banks would soften the plane's landing. On December 17, 1903, Orville Wright piloted the first machine-powered flight in the history of the world. He was airborne for 12 seconds and flew 120 feet, achieving what men and women had dreamed of for centuries—first flight.

# TRUTH OR DARE

Roanoke Island, North Carolina was the site of the first English colony in America. Virginia Dare, born on August 18, 1587, was the first child of English parents to be born on American soil. She was the granddaughter of John White, the governor of the colony, who is famous for his series of paintings of Native American life. Just nine days after her birth, White returned to England for supplies. His journey back to Roanoke Island was delayed for three years because a fleet of Spanish ships was blocking all English ports.

When he finally arrived in 1590, his family and the rest of the colonists had vanished. White and his crew searched everywhere, but the only clue to the settlers' disappearance was the word "Croatoan" carved into a tree on the beach. Some people believe the colonists went north to live with the friendly Croatoan Indians, others believe they were the victims of hurricane, drought, disease, or Native American attack. Although there are many theories, the mystery of the "lost colony" has never been solved.

# WALK THE PLANK!

Blackbeard, one of the most dreaded pirates who ever lived, made a home base in North Carolina, near a string of islands called the Outer Banks. He and his crew of pirates terrorized sailors on the Atlantic Ocean and Caribbean Sea from 1716 to 1718, attacking ships, holding passengers hostage, and stealing anything valuable. Blackbeard's real name was Edward Teach; as his reputation grew, so did his beard and his hair. He began calling himself Blackbeard, braiding his beard and tying the ends with black ribbons to make himself look even more ferocious. His two-year reign of fear came to a bloody end after a surprise attack launched by the governor of Virginia. However, the secret of Blackbeard's buried treasure died with him. To this day, no one has ever found the booty.

# LET THERE BE LIGHT

Cape Hatteras is the largest lighthouse ever to be moved due to erosion problems.

# RHODE ISLAND

**Capital:** Providence

**State Flower:** Violet

**State Tree:** Red Maple

**State Bird:** Rhode Island Red

**Land Area:** 1,045 sq. mi.

Rhode Island's quarter honors Narragansett Bay, the state's largest harbor.

**Rank in Size (Land Area):** 50th

**State Song:** "It's for Me Rhode Island, It's for Me"

**Largest City:** Providence

**Statehood Date:** May 29, 1790

**Nickname:** Ocean State

**Rhode Island gets its name from the Dutch words for "red clay."**

# RHODE ISLAND: HOPE

Italian navigator Giovanni da Verrazano sailed into Narragansett Bay in 1524, becoming the first European to explore Rhode Island. Some people credit him with naming the state, saying he compared Block Island to the island of Rhodes in the Mediterranean.

Others believe it was the Dutch navigator Adriaen Block who came up with the name. He explored Aquidneck Island and the coastal areas of the mainland in 1614. Upon first laying eyes on the red clay of the island's shores, he began calling it *Roodt Eylandt*, meaning Red Island in Dutch. The English pronunciation of this name was Rhode Island. The state's official name is actually The State of Rhode Island and Providence Plantations. Although it is the smallest state in the Union, at 1,045 square miles, it has the longest name of all the states! The origin of this name dates back to 1636, when Roger Williams founded the first settlement, Providence Plantations, on the site of today's capital. For this reason, Rhode Island is sometimes called "The Plantation State." However, the official state nickname is "The Ocean State" because of its 400 miles of beautiful coastline and 100 sandy beaches.

## THE OCEAN STATE

In tribute to the Ocean State, the Rhode Island quarter portrays a vintage sailboat gliding through the Narragansett Bay with the Pell Bridge in the background. Narragansett Bay is an estuary. Estuaries are formed when fresh water from rivers and streams mixes

with salt water. It is a playground for hundreds of species, including lobster, flounder, clams, eelgrass, seals, and people.

Narragansett Bay has a number of different habitats, or places where plants and animals live. These include salt marshes, which act as nurseries for 63 species of fish; fish runs, which provide places for certain types of fish to return from the ocean and spawn in the rivers and streams; and eelgrass, which is a main source of food for marine plants and animals. Eelgrass was once used to insulate homes and to preserve fish before refrigerators were invented. In the last 20 years, major efforts have been made to save these natural ecosystems from the destruction caused by pollution.

Although Rhode Island is only 37 miles long and 48 miles wide, Narragansett Bay's shoreline runs for 400 miles. It has been a seafaring state since colonial times. The old-fashioned sailboat depicted on the new quarter heralds Rhode Island's age-old nautical tradition that is still important to the Ocean State today.

# DIVINE PROVIDENCE

Roger Williams founded the first permanent white settlement in Rhode Island in 1636. A Puritan clergyman, he was expelled from the Massachusetts Bay Colony because of his beliefs in religious and political freedom. After narrowly escaping deportation by the authorities, he journeyed to Narragansett Bay and purchased land from the Narragansett chief Canonicus and his nephew Miantonomo. Williams chose to name the town Providence (now the state capital) because he felt that it was God's merciful providence that sent him there.

Unlike many colonial leaders, Roger Williams always dealt fairly and honestly with the Native Americans. He studied their language and even published a book called *A Key into the Language of America*. In return, the Narragansett respected him and treated him kindly. More settlers came, and under Williams's leadership, they formed a pure democracy with total religious liberty. As a result of this liberal environment, Rhode Island was the first colony to host a Baptist church, a Jewish synagogue, and one of the first Quaker meeting houses.

# SUMMER COTTAGES

Vacationers have been attracted to the cool seashores of Rhode Island for more than 200 years. Newport, one of the oldest resorts in the country, has been around since the colonial period, playing host to some of the nation's richest families. During the Guilded Age, around the turn of the twentieth century, these wealthy families built extravagant oceanfront mansions on the bluffs overlooking Narragansett Bay.

The Breakers, completed in 1895, was the largest, most opulent summer-house of its time, with 70 rooms decorated by an international team of artists and craftsmen. It was designed by Richard Morris Hunt, one of the founding fathers of American architecture, for the Vanderbilt family. Cornelius Vanderbilt had amassed an enormous fortune in the steamship and railroad business. The Breakers stands as a testament to the social and financial importance of the Vanderbilt family at the turn of the 20th century.

# FLYING HORSES

Built in 1876, the Flying Horse Carousel in Watch Hill, Rhode Island, is the oldest carousel in the United States.

# VERMONT

**Capital:** Montpelier

**State Flower:** Red Clover

**State Tree:** Sugar Maple

**State Bird:** Hermit Thrush

**Land Area:** 9,249 sq. mi.

**Rank in Size (Land Area):** 43rd

**State Song:** "Hail Vermont"

**Largest City:** Montpelier

**Statehood Date:** March 4, 1791

**Nickname:** Green Mountain State

**Vermont's name from the French words for "Green Mountain."**

Vermont's quarter portrays a man tapping sugar maples for sap on a windy winter day.

# VERMONT: FREEDOM AND UNITY

Tucked away in the northeast corner of America, Vermont was originally inhabited by a variety of Native Americans from the Algonquin, Iroquois, and Abenaki tribes. French explorer Samuel de Champlain was the first European to discover the region in 1609, while sailing the lake that now bears his name. The name "Vermont" also comes from the French. Upon seeing the lush mountains that form the backbone of the state, these early settlers called them *les verts mont*, meaning "the green mountains." (They must have arrived in the summer months when snow no longer covered the peaks.) Eventually the name was shortened to Verts Mont and then to Vermont, as the English settlers found this easier to pronounce.

Vermont's nickname, "The Green Mountain State," honors this long north-south mountain range that divides the land. It also commemorates the valor and independence of the Green Mountain Boys, a small local militia with a lot of conviction. Under patriot Ethan Allen's leadership, this ragtag bunch of farmers earned a reputation for their prowess in battle. At first they took up arms in defense of their land, which neighboring colonies were unfairly trying to claim. Then they joined forces with all of the colonies to defend American independence, and won a number of decisive battles against the British during the

Revolutionary War. Vermont's motto, "Freedom and Unity," hails the state's long-standing tradition of independence.

## GONE SUGARIN'

The Vermont quarter celebrates the state's most endearing characteristics—its independent spirit, splendid mountains, and beloved maple trees. The reverse (or tail side) of the new quarter features two maple trees being tapped. Not only is the Sugar Maple the state tree of Vermont, but maple—as in maple syrup—is the official state flavor. In late winter and early spring when the ground is usually snow-covered, Vermonters go "sugaring." They collect the sap from the maple trees in a sugarbush, and then boil it in sugarhouses to make syrup. The state produces an average of 400,000 gallons of maple syrup each year. There is nothing quite so delicious as Vermont maple syrup poured over hot pancakes.

In the fall, the Sugar Maple's leaves turn a brilliant red or yellow color. "Leaf peepers" from miles around drive to Vermont just to take in the glorious fall foliage.

Another feature that attracts many visitors to the state are the Green Mountains. Camel's Hump, the mountain featured on the new quarter beside the state motto, "Freedom and Unity," is particularly popular. The Waubanaukee Indians called it Tah-wak-be-dee-ee-wadso, meaning "the saddle mountain," because of its distinctive shape. In 1798, Ira Allen referred to the mountain as "Camel's Rump" on a historical map. From that name, Zadock Thompson came up with "Camel's Hump" in 1830. Today, the mountain is a favorite among hikers—between 10,000 and 15,000 people visit Camel's Hump each year.

## FREEMAN'S OATH

Vermont's sense of independence runs deep. In 1777, Vermont became an independent republic and drafted what was perhaps the most progressive constitution in the world at the time. Not only was it the first to abolish slavery, but also it gave every man the right to vote, regardless of property ownership. (Women, however, were still prohibited from voting at this time.) The right to vote is the most powerful right we have in our country. Each citizen has the opportunity to choose the leader who is best suited to make the rules for the nation and for the state. Vermonters take this responsibility seriously. To this day, residents of the state must take the "Freeman's Oath" before they are able to vote. This pledge, now called the "Voter's Oath," requires individuals to put aside any private wishes or desires, and to vote for the candidate they think is best for the common good.

# GIVE ME SHELTER

There are 106 covered bridges dotting the Vermont countryside. Picturesque and sentimental, they recall a time when life was simpler and connect us to our past. Bridges were often covered during the 19th century to protect the wooden trusses that held them together from the damaging effects of the wind, sun, and rain. With the trusses sheltered, a covered bridge lasted ten times longer than one that had been weather-beaten.

Covered bridges also protected people from the elements. Vermonters used them for many different purposes—trout fishing, military drills on rainy days, kissing in the privacy of horse and buggies, even square dancing. The longest wooden bridge in the United States—465 feet long—spans the Connecticut River, connecting Cornish, New Hampshire, to Windsor, Vermont.

# "SNOWFLAKE" BENTLEY

Have you ever tried to catch a snowflake in your mitten or on your tongue? Wilson A. Bentley of Jericho, Vermont, made capturing snowflakes his lifelong passion—except he used a microscope and a camera. Born in 1865, Bentley developed a scientific curiosity about snowflakes at an early age. He began catching them on a cold, velvet-covered board and photographing them through a microscope in a refrigerated camera room. For years he studied the composition of snow crystals, noting that they were usually six-sided with the occasional three-sided flake. In all his years of careful observation and scientific study, Bentley never found two snowflakes that were the same.

# SMELLY FEET

Montpelier hosts the annual Rotten Sneaker Competition every spring. Judges consider the tongue, the sole, and the smell of each entry to find the stinkiest shoe.

# KENTUCKY

**Capital:** Frankfort

**State Flower:** Goldenrod

**State Tree:** Kentucky Coffeetree

**State Bird:** Cardinal

**Land Area:** 39,732 sq. mi.

**Rank in Size (Land Area):** 36th

**State Song:** "My Old Kentucky Home"

**Largest City:** Frankfort

**Statehood Date:** June 1, 1792

**Nickname:** Bluegrass State

**Kentucky is named for the Iroquois word meaning "land of tomorrow."**

The state song is reflected in this image of a hilltop manor house with a horse grazing on the front lawn.

# KENTUCKY: UNITED WE STAND, DIVIDED WE FALL

Kentucky is one of four states that bear the name "commonwealth." Commonwealths are states governed by the common consent of the people. The term first came into use in mid-17th century England, when Oliver Cromwell ruled the land. As such, it makes sense that the other American commonwealths, Pennsylvania, Massachusetts, and Virginia, were once British colonies. Kentucky originally formed part of Virginia, and upon becoming the 15th state to enter the Union in 1792, it chose to remain a commonwealth. The state's full title is actually the Commonwealth of Kentucky.

Although French and English explorers both visited Kentucky during the 17th century, it was not settled until much later. The Cherokee Indians were the principal occupants of the land, and the name of the state actually comes from the Cherokee word for "meadowland." When early pioneers heard of the fertile meadowlands in central Kentucky, they decided to venture west. There they discovered pastures filled with bluegrass. Bluegrass is not really blue, as the name suggests—it's green. But in the spring, little bluish-purple buds sprout from the grass, giving the fields a bluish hue when seen from a distance. Traders began asking for the seeds of this famed "blue grass of Kentucky," and the state's nickname, "The Bluegrass State," was born.

# GIDDYAP!

Kentucky is most famous for its horse breeding and horse racing. To herald these age-old traditions, the new quarter features a thoroughbred horse standing behind a picket fence. On the first Saturday in May, ever since 1875, people gather at Churchill Downs in Louisville, Kentucky, to watch the best three-year-old thoroughbreds in America race in the Kentucky Derby. It is

the best known horse race in the world and has played a central role in the history of the state. Right from the start, the Derby's commercial success sparked a renewed interest in horse racing and showcased the thoroughbred breeding industry for which Kentucky is famous.

The Kentucky quarter also highlights Federal Hill, the splendid mansion on the Rowan estate that was the inspiration for "My Old Kentucky Home," the state song of Kentucky. Built in 1818 for the distinguished Judge John Rowan, Federal Hill played host to some of the most celebrated personalities of the day, including politicians Henry Clay and Aaron Burr. In 1852, Stephen Foster paid a visit to Federal Hill to see his cousins, the Rowans. It was this visit that inspired him to write the ballad "My Old Kentucky Home," which is commemorated on the new quarter.

# THE WILD FRONTIER

Some of the most legendary figures in America are woven into the fabric of Kentucky history. One such person was frontiersman Daniel Boone. Born and raised in Pennsylvania, Boone achieved lasting fame guiding settlers to the Kentucky frontier and defending them against Native American attack. He was a "long hunter," so named because he took extended hunting trips, exploring the vast landscape of the west along the way. Boone blazed trails and land-hungry settlers followed. In 1775, he led a group of pioneers through the Cumberland Gap along the Wilderness Road to Boonesborough, where he established the first permanent settlement in Kentucky.

# BROTHER AGAINST BROTHER

The first and only president of the Confederate States of America, Jefferson Davis was born on June 3, 1808, in Todd County, Kentucky. Just eight months later, not more than 100 miles away, Abraham Lincoln, who grew up to become the 16th president of the United States, was born in Hardin County. The two men became adversaries during the Civil War, as Lincoln struggled to preserve the Union and Davis fought to uphold the ideals of the South.

Both were brilliant politicians and eloquent statesmen. As the principal spokesman for the southern point of view, Jefferson Davis led the Confederacy energetically and with conviction. Abraham Lincoln, whose Union forces eventually defeated Davis's army, was a humane and far-sighted leader. One of the greatest American presidents in history, he abolished slavery, reunited the war-torn country, and led by example with powerful words and thoughtful deeds.

# HAPPY BIRTHDAY!

The most well known and frequently sung song—"Happy Birthday To You"—was composed by two sisters from Louisville.

50 STATE QUARTERS™

© 1998 U.S.MINT

# PROGRAM

Founded by an act of Congress on April 2, 1792, the United States Mint has been operating for more than 200 years. The Mint produces between 14 and 20 billion circulating coins annually, as well as gold, silver, and platinum coins, proof coins and medals.

The first Mint was constructed in Philadelphia, Pennsylvania. Coins have been produced at this location since 1793. Since this was our only mint for many years, no mint mark was used until 1979 (except on 1942-1945 nickels). Still today the absence of a mint mark designates a coin as a product of the Philadelphia Mint, although a few coins including the quarters of the 50 State Quarters™ Program series do include a "P" mint mark. All engraving for U.S. coins is done at the Philadelphia Mint.

The Philadelphia Mint was our only mint until 1838 when the Dahlonega, Georgia (gold coins only), Charlotte, North Carolina (gold coins only), and New Orleans, Louisiana, mints were established. Later, the Carson City, Denver, San Francisco, and West Point mints were created.

For more information about the U.S. Mint, visit www.USMINT.gov.